REPORT

OF THE

COMMITTEE ON IMPROVEMENT

OF THE

MISSISSIPPI RIVER

AND TRIBUTARIES.

St. Louis, 15th December, 1865.

ST. LOUIS:

GEORGE KNAPP & CO., PRINTERS AND BINDERS.

1865.

REPORT OF COMMITTEE.

St. Louis, Dec. 15, 1865.

The President and Directors of the
Union Merchants' Exchange of St. Louis.

Your Committee have the honor to report that a number of the most populous and thriving cities on the Ohio and Mississippi rivers have been visited; that we find the movement we inaugurated meets with most hearty approval, the advisability of improving navigation on the Mississippi and its tributaries being apparent to all who have interests in that part of the Union permeated by the Mississippi and its affluents. When the main river was closed to commerce, railroads were insufficient for the transportation demanded; the cost of carriage to the sea-board then, and even now, is a severe burden on our surplus produce shipped to Atlantic and foreign ports, the cost of transportation between the producer and consumer eventually and always falling on the producer. To us, cheap water carriage to New Orleans is an inestimable benefit.

The vessels being wholly built and owned among us, their expenses for hands, fuel and repairs, are almost wholly disbursed among the people who support them; no interest on bonds or mortgages, dividends of profits, floats from their earnings to enrich foreign capitalists, the direct producer having a large proportion indirectly returned to him in the disbursements of those employed in navigation for the support of themselves and families.

The rates of freight for the existing year have ruled high from a deficient supply of good and sound vessels, the scarcity of skilled hands, the high price of fuel, and the enhanced first cost of the vessels employed. Competition will, in good time, bring these points to their fair level.

It is the direct interest of the community to cheapen carriage. To facilitate navigation and render it safer, is to reduce the price of transportation without injuring the interest of the carrier; a marine loss of property is a loss of wealth to the community at large; if insured, a percentage has to be paid for the risk incurred; the loss is simply divided by the shareholders of Insurance Companies, instead of falling wholly on the owner. Render navigation more safe, and insurance premiums will be correspondingly lower.

There are tugs now running, which, when the lower river is cleared of snags and similar obstructions, are able at a fair stage of water to take down safely as an ordinary trip, in barges or lighters, from 7,500 to 9,500 tons, or 250,000 to 300,000 bushels of bulk wheat; their complete crew being 31 to 33 hands, all told. This incontestible fact commends itself to the serious notice of the community; the wastage, with ordinary care, is nominal; often the percentage is .001 to .005.

It is proposed to petition Congress through our Representatives to build, equip, and maintain Snag Boats, to remove wrecks, logs and patches of rock from the main channel of the river; to fell timber at falling-in banks; to improve by dam and lock, or otherwise, the rapids of the Mississippi; to improve Grand Chain, on the Ohio, and any other judicious enterprise which may be advisable. Government has at Washington a hydrographic survey of both rapids of the Mississippi; a terrene survey, to estimate the cost of canaling, should, at the earliest moment, be made. If carried out, a fair toll for locking should be collected till the cost and its interest be cancelled.

The whole movement should be under the management of efficient and skilled parties; politics having nothing at stake in this movement, the Superintendent, Captains and superior acting officers should be appointed by the United States authorities, solely from persons recommended annually by a delegation from the Boards of Trade of each port of registration; the tonnage represented being the basis of votes cast; said Board having the power to remove inefficient or unworthy appointees.

The sum total of losses occasioned by obstructions in the Western rivers we are not able to fully state; however, we are assured from sources we deem reliable, that losses by obstructions and detentions on the Mississippi river and tributaries have exceeded three millions of dollars the past year; and further, that the losses by detention and accidents on the lower rapids at Keokuk, will alone for this year exceed half a million of dollars; boats are sometimes three to five days working over them, the difficult part being by the course of the channel but eight miles. Again, that boats during low water, full half the nights lay to at Grand Chain on the Ohio, where four wrecks lay; and still further, there are three or more rocks in the Mississippi river, at its junction with the Ohio, which have been the cause of more than one million dollars losses within the last ten years; bear in mind that these losses to carriers must be repaid by increased rates of freight.

These are but losses of property. The aggregate loss of life may be put down at thousands, comprising every age, sex and condition; lives as valuable to the country as the lives lost on salt water. The duty of Congress on this point is manifest and plain.

The amount of vessels and tonnage now employed on these waters is shown in the following Exhibit, the carrying capacity being the closest test of their value to their owners and the public; the absurd official rule of measuring the engine room, an appurtenance above all caulked seams, sides, deck and plank-shears, rendering the registered tonnage too vague and uncertain to base estimates upon for commercial calculation.

The number of Barges, Lighters and similar craft used as auxiliaries is very large; but the enrolling of such being a new though advisable regulation, the compilation of same was not carried out. The Custom House Collectors were by no means able to enforce the enrollment of very many craft used by Tugs or private individuals. We hope that all craft used as common carriers will in future be licensed, enrolled and undergo inspection.

EXHIBIT A.

PORTS.	No. of Steamers.	Registered Tonnage.	Carrying Capacity.	Value in Dollars.
*Cairo	......	....	......	......
Cincinnati	150	30,497.16	42,983	4,134,000
Dubuque	20	3,204.37	5,137	459,500
Evansville	25	3,043.51	5,019	402,600
Galena	20	2,297.77	3,305	435,000
Keokuk	15	1,173.86	2,192	178,500
Louisville	66	14,100.64	25,425	1,994,500
Memphis	60	9,849.62	15,121	1,011,200
*New Albany	...	....	......	......
Nashville	12	1,183.06	2,156	108,000
*Natchez	...	....	......	......
New Orleans	80	15,860.07	21,625	1,292,000
Paducah	10	2,100.80	2,893	265,000
Pittsburgh, (81 Tugs)	159	33,598.00	42,471	3,920,800
*Quincy	...	....	......	......
St. Paul	39	3,088.52	4,973	607,500
St. Louis	210	86,532.34	110,769	8,830,000
*Vicksburg	...	....	......	......
Wheeling	44	9,538.11	8,075	918,000
	910	216,067.83	292,144	24,556,600

* No registration at these ports for want of local Inspectors.

During the late Rebellion the number and tonnage of steamers has been greatly reduced by various causes incident thereto; though the number of the fleet is rapidly increasing, their aggregate value and freights earned will not progress in the same ratio; we therefore consider it prudent to keep the estimates of revenue below the present minimum value. To say—

We estimate freights earned during 1865, at..........	$32,516,585
Underwriters' valuation of Steamers at 40 per cent. less than their present market value..................................	14,733,960

Levy a tax of 2 per ct. to be collected and added to the freight bill of the consignee, to be paid periodically by the Boats to the Custom House, would produce a revenue of	$650,331
Add 3 per cent. tax on Underwriters' valuation of vessels; annually levied, produces, say..................................	442,018
Nett annual revenue..............	$1,092,349

The tax on Barges, Lighters, &c., will greatly enlarge the above revenue.

To show by example the vast extent of commerce transacted on these waters, we submit the statistics of a few of the cities—all, in fact, we were able to attain—most western cities keeping no public record of their business transacted, the late war having materially affected commerce in our section, and generally disorganized the usual course of trade. You will note the meagre number of cities of importance herein represented, and judge from that how vast will be the aggregate amount of commerce transacted a few years hence, for which we should promptly provide facilities.

Our neighbors in the South have literally next to nothing to show; but with their rich lands and genial winters, there is a great future for them as well as for us; the busy hum of commerce will again ring in the now languid streets and on the wharves of New Orleans.

Congress can devise no more rapid and certain mode of cancelling the public debt, than by fostering the interests and enterprise of the Mississippi valley, whose exports are almost wholly the means of paying foreign imports into the United States.

Let us have free navigation—free from rocks, snags, sunken wrecks and other obstructions in the main channel, from head-waters to the ocean; render it safe and profitable for Tugs to tow a fleet of bulk grain Barges down, salt in bulk and other coarse goods up stream, then in good time freights will be but one-third of the present rates; no measure will tend so much to enrich the country and make it permanently prosperous.

Congress alone having the jurisdiction, let that body approve our measures, give their sanction and authority, and we will raise the necessary revenue out of the class it most directly benefits, without preying on the national coffers.

The Chinese, 2,000 years ago, carried out a vast system of internal navigation, the benefits of which remain to this day. Let us not be behind that semi-barbarous nation in enterprise and sound judicious policy.

If the few towns herein represented have, in 1865, transacted the appended amount of commerce, what will and must be the aggregate of all commerce in the Mississippi valley a few years hence?

IMPORTS, ST. LOUIS, 1865.

ARTICLES.	*Pkgs., &c.*	*Per River.*	*Other Sources.*	*Total.*	*Total Value in Dollars.*
Apples	brls.	64,135	33,684	97,819	$ 342,366
Bacon	casks	7,254	2,638	9,892	1,731,100
"	pcs.	22,023	31,387	53,410	226,992
Bagging	"	3,200	3,911	7,111	199,108
Barley	bush.	751,858	104,069	855,927	1,069,909
Beans	"	16,255	7,168	23,423	46,846
Beef	brls. & tcs.	2,329	349	2,678	48,204
Bran	lbs.	4,247,500	960,000	5,207,500	46,867
Brooms	doz.	9,758	5,948	15,706	62,824
Broom Corn	bales.	839	244	1,083	33,844
Bread	bxs.	20,963	620	21,583	70,145
Butter	lbs.	737,295	1,477,450	2,214,745	664,423
Buckwheat	sks.	229	335	564	1,903
Cattle	head.	19,990	128,674	148,664	8,027,856
Castor Beans	bush.	15,960	12,386	28,346	99,211
Cement	brls.	14,633	576	15,209	64,638
Cider	"	200	297	497	7,455
Coffee	sks.	300	61,000	61,300	3,248,900
Cooperage Flour	brls.	17,282	5,450	22,732	17,049
Pork	"	22,566	3,350	25,916	51,832
Whisky	"	1,486	550	2,036	4,581
Oil	"	1,825	222	2,047	5,322
Lard	tcs.	4,846	1,300	6,146	15,365
Corn	bush.	2,400,000	682,746	3,082,746	2.774,471
Cornmeal	sks.	3,133	151	3,284	7,389
"	brls.	20,252	1,593	21,845	98,302
Cotton	bales	86,000	1,885	87.885	19,774,125
Cheese	bxs.	553	41,575	42,128	379,152
Dried Fruit	sks.	4,635	8,734	13,369	34,091
"	brls.	3,426	2,151	5,577	16,452
Eggs	pkgs.	6,347	3,776	10,123	103,950
Flaxseed	bush.	16,537	27,750	44,287	88,574
Fish	brls.	6,280	9,101	15,381	230.715
"	kitts	8,750	69,100	77,850	194,625
Flour	brls.	461,200	513,390	974,590	9,745,900
Furs, Buff.	bales	5,981	515	6,496	779,520
" and Peltries	pkgs., &c.	570	704	1,274	200,000
Grease	brls.	773	351	1,124	42,712
Gunnies	bales	1,509	3,823	5,332	466,550
"	bdls.	7,655	713	8,368	104,600
Hair	sks.	3,446	1,680	5,126	12,302
Hay	bales	136,880	124,634	261,514	1,144,124
Hemp	"	36,163	3,075	39,238	1,177,140
Hides	pcs.	131,000	68,000	199,000	509,440
Horses and Mules	head	61,573	......	61,573	6,957,749
Hogs (estim'd)	"	21,136	184,203	205,339	5,133,475
Iron	bdls. & pcs.	140,720	21,288	162,008	733,896
Lard	tcs. & brls.	16,844	2,235	19,079	1,201,977
"	kegs.	1,972	......	1,972	20,706
"	pkgs.	2,296	1,378	3,674	169,004
Lead	pigs	44,000	64,633	108,633	754,999

Imports, St. Louis, 1865 (concluded).

ARTICLES.	*Pkgs., &c.*	*Per River.*	*Other Sources.*	*Total.*	*Total Value in Dollars.*
Leather	rolls	3,800	18,726	22,526	$ 1,013,670
Lemons	bxs.	1,460	121	1,581	18,972
Lye	cases	2,310	395	2,705	32,460
Lumber	per M ft.	75,000,000	13,152,000	88,152,000	1,851,192
" square and log	" "	30,000,000	......	30,000,000	450,000
Lime	brls.	4,000	592	4,592	9,184
Malt	sks.	4,000	40,000	44,000	176,000
Molasses	brls.	8,000	4,422	12,422	621,100
Nails	kegs	67,730	18,320	86,050	645,375
Oats	bush.	3,370,457	650,210	4,020,677	2,412,400
Oils	brls.	15,308	21,684	36,992	2,663,424
Oakum	bales		3,020	3,020	19,630
Onions	bush.	200,000	859	200,859	401,718
Oranges	bxs.	1,518	64	1,582	15,820
Paper	bdls.	22,667	283,333	306,000	1,683,000
Pig Iron	tons	21,500	15,727	37,227	2,121,939
Pork	brls.	60,456	3,800	64,256	1,927,680
"	casks	10,623	582	11,205	1,568,700
"	bxs.	4,188	650	4,838	388,660
"	pcs.	307,600	26,000	333,600	1,251,000
Potatoes	bush.	478,156	83,741	561,897	561,897
Rags	pkgs.	10,346	6,065	16,411	82,055
Rope—10 ft. per lb., 17 lbs. fair	coils	2,482	8,044	10,526	492,490
Raisins	bxs.	1,984	8,492	10,476	62,856
Rye	bush.	189,790	8,200	197,990	138,593
Salt	sks.	68,863	11,866	80,729	242,187
"	brls.	141,678	26,600	168,278	504,834
Seed	sks.	4,529	3,311	7,840	351,180 (sks. and brls.)
"	brls.	2,542	1,324	3,866	
Sheep	head	13,765	81,148	94,913	417,617
Shipstuff	lbs.	348,200	25,500	373,700	448,440
Shingles	per M.	298,000		298,000	1,490,000
Soap	bxs.	2,377	411	1,788	8,940
Spikes	kegs	395	270	665	5,154
Springs	pcs.	1,033	175	1,208	10,268
Starch	bxs.	6,354	10,500	16,854	73,315
Steel	pcs.	11,367	251	11,618	95,848
Soda Ash, &c.	tons	1,250		1,250	187,500
Sugar	hhds.	9,040	8,505	17,545	3,684,450
"	brls.	1,453	6,505	7,958	358,110
"	bxs.	21,621	6,404	28,025	1,681,500
Tallow	brls.	5,800	4,631	10,431	187,758
Tobacco	hhds.	9,654	6,698	16,352	3,270,400
"	bxs. & pkgs.	12,060	9,655	21,715	760,025
Wheat	bush.	3,000,000	507,980	3,507,980	7,015,760
Whiskey	brls.	25,000	8,249	33,249	3,067,220
Wines	"	1,233	566	1,799	287,840
"	baskets	1,954	645	2,599	72,772
Window-glass	bxs.	11,786	224	12,010	73,862
Wool	bales	6,578	3,805	10,383	2,076,600
				143,167,326	
Sundries and unclassified Merchandise		......	......	......	120,000,000
					235,873,875

PACKAGES AND VALUE OF LEADING IMPORTS.

ARTICLES. *pkgs.*	CINCINNATI.		LOUISVILLE.		TOTALS.	
	Pkgs.	*Value in Dolls.*	*Pkgs.*	*Value in Dolls.*	*Pkgs.*	*Value in Dolls.*
Apples ......brls.	189,539	606,525	21,556	150,992	211,095	757,517
" dried and Peaches.pkgs.	50,624	108,310	....	......	50,624	108,310
Ale, Beer and Porter .... brls.	10,933	98,397	....	......	10,933	98,397
Buff. Bobes .bales	45	4,050	...	......	45	4,05[illegible]
Bagging ..... pcs.	594	9,504	11,504	345,030	12,098	354,534
Barley......bush.	542,712	700,098	178,670	223,348	721,382	923,446
Beans ...... "	92,308	184.618	....	......	92,308	184,618
Beef.........brls.	6,710	134,200	....	......	6,710	134,200
" .... tcs.	2,138	64,140	....	......	2,138	64,140
Blooms......tons	550	60,500	....	......	550	60,500
Bran, Shipstuff, &c......... sks.	178,917	256,808	....	......	178,917	256,808
Butter......pkgs.	62,209	1,418,697	10,005	400,200	72,214	1.818,897
Bale Rope...coils	....	......	9,206	142,693	9,206	142,693
Boots and Shoes .....cases	23,875	1,910,000	....	......	23,875	1,910,009
Coal........bush.	16,000,000	3,200,000	13,536,250	3,384,462	29,536,250	6,584,062
Cattle ...... head	54 424	4,353,290	77,169	4,630,140	131,593	8,983,430
Cement and Plaster ....brls.	25,966	97 372	....	......	25,966	97,372
Cheese ..... pkgs.	125,910	693,460	31,600	379,200	157,510	1,072,660
Cider........ brls.	7,718	77,180	. ..	......	7,718	77,180
Coffee ....sks.	173,792	9,819,248	37,698	1,884,900	211,490	11,704,148
Cooperage, pcs., &c.	173,927	361,319	....	......	173,927	361,319
Corn .... bush.	1,262,198	984,514	555,510	388,167	1,817,708	1,372,681
Corn Meal ..pkgs.	7,767	6,990	....	......	7,767	6,990
Cotton ..... bales	88,472	23,002,720	36,403	9,100,750	124,875	32,103,470
Cotton Yarn, &c........pkgs.	19,565	129,156	9,294	371,760	28,869	500,916
Crockery Ware ....crates	4,051	567,140	....	......	4,051	567,140
Candles......bxs.	6,835	54,680	11,372	142,140	18,207	196,820
Drugs ......pkgs.	....	......	41,985	1,225,000	41,985	1,225,000
Eggs .... pkgs.	22,162	155,134	4,000	100,000	26,162	255,134
Flaxseed ...pkgs.	34,082	240,894	11,700	58,500	45,782	299,394
Feathers .....sks.	6,968	278,720	....	......	6,968	278,720
Fish ....brls.	36,503	562,865	....	......	36,503	562,865
" .... kitts, &c.	106,477	305,129	....	......	106,477	305,129
Flour........brls.	671,570	5,238,246	100,620	1,006,200	772,190	6,244,446
Fruits ......pkgs.	....	......	68,722	687,720	68,722	687,720
Grease .....pkgs.	14,630	395,010	....	......	14,630	395,010
Glass (Window).......bxs.	62,493	344,211	....	......	62,493	344,211
Glassware ..pkgs.	44,150	393,800	....	......	44,150	393,800
Hay ....bales	118,194	271,846	105,600	316,800	223,794	588,646
Hardware, pcs. & pkgs.	22,515	5,178,450	249,884	2,498,840	272,399	7,677,290
Hemp ...... bales	11,864	1,423,680	10,404	468,180	22,268	1,891,860
Hides.bdls. & pcs.	226,349	1,244,919	51,825	248,705	278,174	1,493,619
" .... lbs.	52,803	4,752	....	......	52,803	4,752
Hogs........head	435,468	11,322,168	48,177	1,734,372	483,645	13,056,540
Horses and Mules.....head	37,433	5,240,620	10,095	1,049,525	47,528	6,290,145
Hops ....pkgs.	3,785	90,840	....	......	3,785	90,840
Iron..pcs. & bdls.	33,319	186,554	....	......	33,919	186,554
" ..slabs & pcs.	113,304	322,916	....	......	113,304	322,916
" ....tons	24,158	3,019,750	....	......	24,158	3,019,750
" Pig......tons	23,467	1,126,416	15,000	750,000	38,467	1,876,416
Lead.........pigs	37,105	482,365	....	......	37,105	482,365
Leather......rolls	29,241	789,507	....	......	29,241	789,537

Packages and Value of leading Imports (concluded).

ARTICLES. *pkgs.*	CINCINNATI.		LOUISVILLE.		TOTALS.	
	Pkgs.	*Value in Dolls.*	*Pkgs.*	*Value in Dolls.*	*Pkgs.*	*Value in Dolls.*
Lemons ......bxs.	808	8,888	....	......	808	8,888
Lard ....tcs.	55,556	3,000,024	2,500	250,000	58,056	3,250,024
" ....kegs, &c.	6,430	57,870	2,611	39,165	9,041	97,035
Lumber ...per M.	50,000,000	1,375,000	3,914,000	174,280	53,914,000	1,549,280
Lime ....brls.	73,020	102,228	....	......	73,020	102,228
Liquor......pkgs.	548	411,000	48,657	2,500,000	49,205	2,911,000
Malt........bush.	179,185	161,265	67,383	107,812	246,568	269,077
Maize.......pkgs.	91,610	91,610,000	519,619	135,604,320	631,229	227,214,320
" ....tons	40,568	73,022,400	1,360,707	......	1,401,275	73,022,400
Molasses and Syrup .... brls.	37,998	1,975,896	39,503	366,975	77,501	2,342,871
Nails & Horse Shoes ......kgs.	157,232	943,392	39,543	221,531	196,775	1,164,923
Oils ....brls.	14,239	996,730	13,911	1,112,680	28,150	2,109,410
Oranges .....bxs.	1,456	14,560	....	......	1,456	14,560
Oats........bush.	2,358,053	1,179,026	282,284	141,246	2,640,337	1,320,272
Oakum .....bales	5,134	184,824	....	......	5,134	184,824
Oilcake......tons	464	30,160	....	......	464	30,160
Onions .....pkgs.	5,434	32,604	....	......	5,434	32,604
Potatoes....bush.	637,667	892,734	144,437	144,437	782,104	1,037,171
Pepper and Pimento, &c. . bgs.	3,890	136,150	....	......	3,890	136,150
Pork and Bacon ..cks. & tcs.	11,728	1,011,995	5,316	664,500	17,044	1,676,495
" ... .brls.	38,642	1,159,260	7,681	251,154	46,323	1,410,414
" .....bxs.	3,026	190,638	....	....	3,026	190,638
" ....pkgs.	543,427	1,521,595	35,200	115,333	578,627	1,636,928
Petroleum ...brls.	50,915	1,120,350	....	......	50,915	1,120,350
Rye..........bush.	190,547	200,074	6,600	5,740	197,147	205,814
Rosin.........brls.	1,124	48,332	....	......	1,124	48.332
Rope and Twine ....pkgs.	17,086	256,290	....	......	17,086	256,290
Rice ....pkgs.	5,140	411,200	....	......	5,140	411,200
Raisins and Figs ....bxs.	31,879	197,650	....	......	31,879	197,650
Sugar ......hhds.	23,017	5,238,825	5,412	1,042,400	28,429	6,281,225
" ...... bxs.	6,125	428,750	....	.....	6,125	428,750
" ...... brls.	86,390	4,319,500	43,476	2,173,800	129,866	6,493,300
Sheep ....head	47,023	178,687	49,020	196,080	96,043	376,767
Salt ....sks.	50,916	244,396	....	... ..	50,916	244,396
" ....brls.	141,990	567,860	124,293	372,380	266,283	940,340
Seed........pkgs.	14.856	445,680	11,720	175,800	26,576	621,480
Soap ....bxs.	....	......	15,895	87,012	15,895	87,012
Starch ....bxs.	55,591	450,159	11,275	13,262	66,866	463,421
Shingles...per M.	170,000	1,105,000	4,085	28,508	174,085	1,133,508
Shot ....kgs.	5,249	199,462	....	......	5,249	199,462
Stearine ......tcs.	2,668	144,072	....	......	2,668	144,072
Tobacco ....hhds.	54,359	14,948,725	43.677	6,519,287	98,036	21,468,012
" bxs & kgs.	22,867	1,372,020	10,809	432,360	33,676	1,804,380
" ....pkgs.	7,447	372,350	....	......	7,447	372,350
Tea ....pkgs.	7,368	884.160	....	... ..	7,368	884,160
Tallow.......brls.	16,932	593,620	....	......	16,932	593,620
Tar & Pitch .brls.	2,769	64,516	....	......	2,769	64,516
Turpentine ..brls.	318	34,980	....	......	318	34,980
Whiskey .... brls.	70,700	6,363,000	20,365	1,823,850	91,065	8,186,850
Wheat......bush.	1,678,395	3,051,110	378,936	757,832	2,057,331	3,808,942
Wool..sks. & bgs.	11,044	662,640	....	......	11,044	662,640
Wines...brls. and pkgs.	4,352	696,320	....	......	4,352	696,320
" bxs. & bask.	5,931	160,299	....	......	5,931	160,299
White Lead..kgs.	....	......	14,096	140,960	14,096	140,960
	78,329,532	312,300,074	22,462,436	187,149,923	100,791,968	499,449,997

STATEMENT OF A FEW LEADING IMPORTS RECEIVED AT

ARTICLES.	FULTON CITY.		LA SALLE.		PRAIRIE DU CHIEN, M'GREGOR AND NORTH M'GREGOR.		WINONA.	
	PACKAGES.	VALUE.	PACKAGES.	VALUE.	PACKAGES.	VALUE.	PACKAGES.	VALUE.
Barley ....bush.	22,604	$ 11,302	942	$ 471	21,351	$ 19,216	....	....
Corn.......................... "	557,143	256,285	2,562,292	1,178,654	732,071	439,243	....	....
Flour ....brls.	....	....	31,136	179,032	43,501	282,757	5,000	$ 30,000
Hardware &c. ....pkgs., &c.	....	....	2,220	44,320	....	....	....	....
Lard...........................tcs.	....	....	1,593	79,581	....	....	....	....
Merchandise.........tons, &c.	2,375	950,000	1,739	695,294	2,641	1,256 464	500	200,000
Oats ....bush.	87,857	23,721	63,864	17,243	878.486	210,837	....	....
Pork ....brls.	....	....	8,730	226,980	....	....	....	....
" .... pcs.	....	....	2,599	119,179	....	....	....	....
Rye ....bush.	....	....	90,980	31,843	....	....	....	....
Seed.......................pkgs.	....	....	11,355	329,295	....	....	....	....
Wheat .... bush.	304,167	334,584	251,872	277,059	2,049,800	2,459,760	2,250,000	2,700,000
	974,146	$1,575,892	3,029,322	$3,178,951	3,727,850	$4,668,277	2,255,000	$2,930,000

STATEMENT OF IMPORTS, 1865.

Articles.	Pkgs., &c.	St. Louis.	Cincinnati.	Louisville.	Fulton City.	La Salle.	Prairie du Chien, McGregor and N. McG.	Winona.	Total Pkgs.	Value.
Apples	brls.	97,819	189,539	21,556	......	....	....	....	308,914	1,099,883
" Dried & Peaches	pkgs.	18,946	50,624	......	......	....	....	....	69,570	158,853
Ale, Beer, Porter	brls.	......	10,933	......	......	....	....	....	10,933	98,397
Buffalo Robes	bales	6,496	45	......	......	....	....	....	6,541	783,570
Bacon	casks & tcs.	9,892	......	......	......	....	....	....	9,892	1,731,100
"	pcs.	53,410	......	......	......	....	....	....	53,410	226,992
Bagging	pcs.	7,111	594	11,504	......	....	....	....	19,209	553,642
Barley	bush.	855,927	542,712	178,670	22,604	942	21,351	....	1,622,206	2,024,344
Beans	"	23,423	92,308	......	......	....	....	....	115,731	231,464
Beef	brls.	2,678	6,710	......	......	....	...	....	9,388	182,404
"	tcs.	......	2,138	......	......	....	....	....	2,138	64,140
Blooms	tons.	......	550	......	......	....	....	....	550	60,500
Bran Ship-stuff	cks.	111,624	178,917	......	......	....	...	....	290,541	752,115
Brooms	doz.	15,706	......	......	......	....	....	....	15,706	62,824
Broom Corn	bales.	1,083	......	......	......	....	....	....	1,083	33,844
Bread and Crackers	pkgs.	21,583	......	......	......	....	....	....	21,583	70,145
Butter	"	34,073	62,209	10,005	......	....	....	....	106,287	2,483,320
Bale Rope	coils	......	......	9,206	......	....	....	....	9,206	142,693
Boots and Shoes	cases	......	23,875	......	......	....	....	....	23,875	1,910,000
Buckwheat	pkgs.	564	......	......	......	....	....	....	564	1,903
Coal	bush.	......	16,000,000	13,536,250	......	....	....	....	29,536,250	6,584,062
Cattle	head	148,664	54,424	77,169	......	....	....	....	280,257	17,011,286
Castor Beans	pkgs.	28,346	......	......	......	....	....	....	28,346	99,211
Cement and Plaster	brls.	15,209	25,966	......	......	....	....	....	41,175	162,010
Cheese	pkgs.	42,128	125,910	31,600	......	....	....	....	199,638	1,451,812
Cider	brls.	497	7,718	......	......	....	....	....	8,215	84,635
Coffee	sks.	61,300	173,792	37,698	......	....	....	....	272,790	14,953,048

Cooperage ...... pcs.	58,877	173,927	......	......	....	....	....	232,804	455,468
Corn ...... bush.	3,082,746	1,262,198	555,510	557,143	2,562,292	732,071	....	8,751,960	6,021,334
Cornmeal ...... pkgs.	25,129	7,767	......	......	....	....	....	32,896	112,681
Cotton ...... bales.	87,885	88,472	36,403	......	....	....	....	212,760	51,877,595
Cotton Yarn, &c. ...... pkgs.	......	19,565	9,294	....	....	....	....	28,859	500,916
Crockery Ware ...... crates	......	4,051	......	......	....	....	....	4,051	567,140
Candles ...... bxs.	......	6,835	11,372	......	....	....	....	18,207	196,820
Drugs ...... pkgs.	......	......	41,985	......	....	....	....	41,985	1,225,000
Eggs ...... "	10,123	22,162	4,000	......	....	....	....	36,285	359,084
Flax Seed ...... pkgs.	7,655	34,082	11,700	......	....	....	....	53,437	387,968
Feathers ...... sks.	......	6,968	......	......	....	....	....	6,968	278,720
Fish ...... brls.	15,381	36,503	......	......	....	....	....	51,884	793,580
" ...... kitts, &c.	77,850	106,477	......	......	....	....	....	184,327	499,754
Flour ...... brls.	974,590	671,570	100,620	......	31,136	43,501	5,000	1,826,417	16,482,135
Furs and Peltries ...... pkgs., &c.	1,274	......	......	......	....	....	....	1,274	200,000
Fruits ...... pkgs.	......	......	68,722	......	....	....	....	68,722	687,720
Grease ...... pkgs.	1,124	14,330	......	......	....	....	....	15,754	437,722
Glass (window) ...... bxs.	12,910	62,493	......	......	....	....	....	74,503	418,073
Glassware ...... pkgs.	......	44,150	......	......	....	....	....	44,150	393,800
Gunnies ...... bales	5,332	......	......	......	....	....	....	5,332	466,550
" ...... bdls.	8,368	......	......	......	....	....	....	8,368	104,600
Hair ...... sks.	5,126	......	......	......	....	....	....	5,126	12,302
Hay ...... bales	261,514	118,194	105.600	......	....	....	....	485,308	1,732,770
Hardware ...... pkgs. & pcs.	......	22,515	249,884	......	2,220	....	....	274,619	7,721,610
Hemp ...... bales	39,238	11,364	10,404	......	....	....	....	61,506	3,069,000
Hides ...... bdls. & pcs.	199,000	226,349	51,825	......	....	....	....	477,174	2,003,059
" ...... lbs.	......	52,803	......	......	....	....	....	52,803	4,752
Hogs ...... head	205,339	435,468	48,177	......	....	....	....	688,984	18,190,015
Horses and Mules ...... "	61,573	37,433	10,095	......	....	....	....	109,101	13,247,894
Hops ...... pkgs.	......	3,785	......	......	....	....	....	3,785	90,840
Iron ...... pcs. & bdls.	162,008	33,919	......	......	....	....	....	195,927	920,450
" ...... slabs & pcs.	......	113,304	......	......	....	....	....	113,304	322,916

Statement of Imports, 1865 (concluded).

ARTICLES.	*Pkgs., &c.*	*St. Louis.*	*Cincinnati.*	*Louisville.*	*Fulton City*	*La Salle.*	Prairie du Chien, Mc-Gregor and N. McG.	*Winona.*	*Total Pkgs.*	*Value.*
Iron	tons	......	24,158	......	....	......	......	......	24,158	3,019,750
" "Pig"	"	37,227	23,467	15,000	....	......	......	......	75,694	3,998,355
Lead	pigs	108,633	37,105	......	....	......	......	......	145,738	1,237,364
Leather	rolls	22,526	29,241	......	....	......	......	......	51,767	1,803,177
Lemons	bxs.	1,581	808	......	....	......	......	......	2,389	27,860
Lard	tcs.	19,079	55,556	2,500	....	1,593	......	......	78,728	4,531,582
"	kegs, &c.	5,646	6,430	2,611	....	......	......	......	14,687	286,745
Lumber	per M.	118,152,000	50,000,000	3,914,000	....	......	......	......	172,066,000	3,850,472
Lye	cases	2,705	......	......	....	......	......	......	2,705	32,460
Lime	brls.	4,592	73,020	......	....	......	......	......	77,612	111,412
Liquor	pkgs.	......	548	48,657	....	......	......	......	49,205	2,911,000
Malt	bush.	110,000	179,185	67,383	....	......	......	......	356,568	445,077
Merchandise	pkgs.	......	91,610	539,619	....	......	......	......	631,229	227,214,320
"	tons	......	40,568	1,360,707	2,375	1,739	2,641	500	1,408,530	196,124,158
Molasses Syrup	brls.	12,422	37,998	14,679	....	......	......	......	65,099	2,963,971
Nails and Horse-shoes	kegs	86,715	157,232	39,543	....	......	......	......	283,490	1,815,452
Oils	brls.	36,992	14,239	13,911	....	......	......	......	65,142	4,772,834
Oranges	bxs.	1,582	1,456	......	....	......	......	......	3,038	30,380
Oats	bush.	4,020,667	2,358,053	282,284	87,857	63,864	878,486	......	7,691,211	3,984,473
Oakum	bales	3,020	5,134	......	....	......	......	......	8,154	204,454
Oil Cake	tons	......	464	......	....	......	......	......	464	30,160
Onions	brls. & sks.	80,344	5,434	......	....	......	......	......	85,778	434,322
Paper	bdls.	306,000	......	......	....	......	......	......	306,000	1,683,000
Potatoes	bush.	561,897	637,667	144,437	....	......	......	......	1,344,001	1,599,068
Pepper, Pimento, &c.	bags	......	3,890	......	....	......	......	......	3,890	136,150
Pork & Bacon	cks., &c.	64,256	11,728	5,316	....	......	......	......	81,300	3,245,195
"	brls.	11,205	38,642	7,681	....	8,730	......	......	66,258	3,565,074
"	bxs.	4,838	3,026	......	....	......	......	......	7,864	529,298
"	pcs.	333,600	543,427	35,200	....	2,599	......	......	914,826	3,007,107
Petrloeum	brls.	......	50,915	......	....	......	......	......	50,915	1,120,350

Rags ...... pkgs.	16,411	......	......	....	......	......	......	16,411	82,055
Rye ...... bush.	197,990	190,547	6,600	....	90,980	......	......	486,117	376,250
Rosin ...... brls.	......	1,124	......	....	......	......	......	1,124	48,332
Rope and Twine ...... pkgs.	10,526	17,086	......	....	......	......	......	27,612	748,380
Rice ...... "	......	5,140	......	....	......	......	......	5,140	411,200
Raisins and Figs ...... bxs.	10,476	31,879	......	....	......	......	......	42,355	260,506
Sugar ...... hhds.	17,545	23,017	5,412	....	......	......	......	45,974	9,965,675
" ...... bxs.	28,025	6,125	......	....	......	......	......	34,150	2,110,250
" ...... brls.	7,958	86,390	43,476	....	......	......	......	137,824	6,851,410
Sheep ...... head	94,913	47,023	49,020	....	......	......	......	190,956	792,384
Salt ...... sks.	80,729	50,916	......	....	......	......	......	131,645	486,583
" ...... brls.	168,278	141,990	124,293	....	......	......	......	434,561	1,445,174
Seed ...... pkgs.	11,706	14,856	11,720	....	11,355	......	......	49,637	1,301,955
Soap ...... bxs.	1,788	......	15,895	....	......	......	......	17,683	95,952
Starch ...... bxs.	16,854	55,591	11,275	....	......	......	......	83,720	536,736
Shingles ...... per M.	298,000	170,000	4,085	....	......	......	......	472,085	2,623,508
Steel ...... pcs., &c.	11,618	......	......	....	......	......	......	11,618	95,848
Springs ...... pcs.	1,208	......	......	....	......	......	......	1,208	10,268
Soda Ash ...... tons.	1,250	......	......	....	......	......	......	1,250	187,500
Shot ...... kegs.	......	5,249	......	....	......	......	......	5,249	199,462
Stearine ...... tcs.	......	2,668	......	....	......	......	......	2,668	144,072
Tobacco ...... hhds.	16,352	54,359	43,677	....	......	......	......	114,388	24,738,412
" ...... bxs. & kegs.	21,715	22,867	10,809	....	......	......	......	55,391	2,564,405
" ...... pkgs.	......	7,447	......	....	......	......	......	7,447	372,350
Tea ...... pkgs.	......	7,368	......	....	......	......	......	7,368	884,160
Tallow ...... brls.	10,431	16,932	......	....	......	......	......	27,363	781,378
Tar and Pitch ...... brls.	......	2,769	......	....	......	......	......	2,769	64.516
Turpentine ...... brls.	......	318	......	....	......	......	......	318	34,980
Whiskey ...... brls.	33,249	70,700	20,365	....	......	......	......	124,314	11,254,070
Wheat ...... bush.	3,507,980	1,678,395	378,936	304,167	251,872	2,049,800	2,250,000	10,421,150	16,596,305
Wool ...... sks. & bags.	10,383	11,044	......	....	......	......	......	21,427	2,739,240
Wines ...... brls. & hf. cks.	1,799	4,352	......	....	......	......	......	6,151	984,160
" ...... bxs. & bask.	2,599	5,931	......	....	......	......	......	8,530	233,071
White Lead ...... kegs.	......	......	14,096	....	......	......	......	14,096	140,960
								246,204,717	$ 747,676,992

It is estimated that a Snag Boat, double or twin hull, 20 feet beam, 180 feet long, with 16 feet space or well, total width 56 feet, 7 feet hold, will cost say, - - - - - - $32,000

Two engines, 20 inch cylinders, 6 feet stroke, with 4 boilers, 2 on each hull..	25,000
Hoisting apparatas, saws, chains, rigging, anchors, outfit, furniture, upper work and incidental charges..............	27,500
	$84,500

A smaller boat, say 160 feet long, 50 feet wide, with appurtenances, would probably cost.. $65,000
Cost of working a Snag Boat per diem..................... $60
Fuel, on an average, " " .... 50 —— 110

It will be understood that steam is only wanted a portion of the time for propelling powerful hoisting apparatus, and all successful machinery that can be economically used should be provided, as well as a Diver and his apparatus; none but capable employees appointed, and they promptly changed when advisable.

From the few statistics we have been able to collect, the public will understand how immense the aggregate would be were we able to obtain from all the towns on western waters, or even more full returns from a part.

We have given but the imports; had we given exports also, possibly a part might have been twice represented.

We have studiously avoided modeling this movement exclusively for St. Louis. It is, we consider, an enterprise intimately connected with the indwellers of the basin of the Mississippi; a movement in which no sectional, no local feelings should be indulged or permitted; a broad generalization, the greatest service to the greatest number, should actuate us, one and all. Let us work together as one body, having one interest, and that interest will be an accomplished fact.

We respectfully urge that all Senators and Representatives in Congress, from the Mississippi valley in particular, as well as all having the interest of our common country at heart, be appealed to for aid and support in this movement, so fraught with benefit to the whole community; one so greatly cheapening the interchange of products of the various States they and we represent.

Very respectfully yours,

GEO. PARTRIDGE, *Chairman.*

David White,
Isaac H. Sturgeon,
D. A. January,
Henry W. Smith,
Jno. N. Bofinger,
Geo. R. Taylor,
W. H. Pulsifer,
Thomas H. Griffith,
James F. Griffith.

At a called meeting of the Board of Directors of the Union Merchants' Exchange, December 20, 1865, B. ABLE, President, in the chair, the Report of the "*Committee on Improvement of Navigation of the Mississippi River and its tributaries*," was read by its Secretary, JAMES F. GRIFFITH.

On motion of ALEX. N. SMITH, it was

Resolved, That the Report be accepted and 500 copies ordered to be printed.

www.ingramcontent.com/pod-product-compliance
Lightning Source LLC
LaVergne TN
LVHW020642110826
845149LV00004B/1322

* 9 7 8 1 4 1 8 1 9 0 7 4 3 *